PowerKids Readers:

Bilingual Edition
My Library of Holidays™
Edición Bilingüe

Daryl Heller
Traducción al español:
Tomás González

The Rosen Publishing Group's
PowerKids Press™ & **Editorial Buenas Letras**™
New York

For Caleigh, Chetham, Elliot, Hana, Harry, and Maxine

Published in 2004 by The Rosen Publishing Group, Inc.
29 East 21st Street, New York, NY 10010

First Edition

Book Design: Michael J. Caroleo

Photo Credits: Cover, pp. 5, 7, 9, 21, 22 (menorah, shamash, temple) © CORBIS; p. 13 © Dex Images, Inc./CORBIS; p. 15 © The Rosen Publishing Group; pp. 17, 22 (Gimel) by Michael Caroleo.

Heller, Daryl
        Hanukkah = Januca / Daryl Heller ; translated by Tomas Gonzalez.
              p. cm. – (My library of holidays)
        Includes bibliographical references and index.
        Summary: This book explains the Jewish history that is the background for Hanukkah and describes how Hanukkah is celebrated.
        ISBN 1-4042-7525-8 (lib.)
        1. Hanukkah–Juvenile literature   [1. Hanukkah
2. Holidays   3. Spanish language materials–Bilingual]
I. Title II. Title: Januca III. Series
        BM695.H3 H4618 2004   2003-009375
        296.4'35–dc21

Manufactured in the United States of America

Contents

Contenido

Long ago, a group of Jews called the Maccabees fought for their beliefs. After winning the fight they returned to their temple. They lit a lamp with a small bit of oil.

Hace mucho tiempo un grupo de judíos llamado los macabeos luchó por sus creencias. Después de ganar la batalla, regresaron a su templo y encendieron una lámpara con una pequeña cantidad de aceite.

4

That tiny bit of oil in the temple lamp burned for eight full days. This is why Jewish people keep the holiday of Hanukkah for eight days. Today Hanukkah candles are lit on a menorah.

Aquella minúscula cantidad de aceite ardió durante ocho días. Es por eso que la fiesta de Jánuca dura ocho días. Hoy, las velas de Jánuca se encienden en candelabros llamados menoras.

Many families gather during Hanukkah. Everyone sits down for a tasty meal.

Durante la fiesta de Jánuca se reúnen muchas familias. Las familias se sientan a disfrutar de una deliciosa cena.

Potato latkes are often served during the holiday. Latkes are shaped like pancakes and are sometimes eaten with applesauce.

Latkes de papa se sirven a menudo durante esta fiesta. Los latkes tienen forma de panqueques y con frecuencia se sirven con salsa de manzana.

Many families give each other gifts after the Hanukkah dinner has been eaten.

Después de disfrutar de la cena de Jánuca, muchas familias intercambian regalos.

13

A dreidel is a top with Hebrew letters printed on it. During Hanukkah it is used to play a game.

Un dreidel es un trompo con letras hebreas impresas. Se juega con él durante la fiesta de Jánuca.

15

These are the Hebrew letters that are printed on a dreidel. If you spin the dreidel and it falls on the letter gimel, you win a pile of candy, pennies, or nuts.

Éstas son las letras hebreas impresas en el dreidel. Si haces girar el dreidel y cae en la letra gimel, ganas un montón de dulces, centavos o nueces.

17

Many children eat candy gelt on Hanukkah. "Gelt" is a word that means "money."

Es frecuente que los niños coman dulces en forma de gelt durante la fiesta de Jánuca. La palabra "gelt" significa "dinero".

19

Each day the *shamash* is used to light the other Hanukkah candles. The shamash is taller than the other candles.

Todos los días se usa la vela *shamash* para encender las otras velas de Jánuca. La vela shamash es más alta que las otras.

21

Words to Know
Palabras que debes saber

applesauce
salsa de manzana

the Hebrew letter gimel
la letra hebrea gimel

menorah
menora

potato latkes
latkes de papa

shamash

temple
templo

Here are more books to read about Hanukkah / Otros libros que puedes leer sobre Jánuca:

In English/En inglés:
The Festival of Lights: The Story of Hanukkah
by Maida Silverman and Carolyn S. Ewing, illustrator

Hershel and the Hanukkah Goblins
by Eric A. Kimmel and Trina Schart Hyman, illustrator

Due to the changing nature of Internet links, PowerKids Press has developed an online list of Web sites related to the subject of this book. This site is updated regularly. Please use this link to access the list:

www.buenasletraslinks.com/hol/jan

Index

Índice

Words in English: 197   Palabras en español: 211

Note to Parents, Teachers, and Librarians

PowerKids Readers books *en español* are specially designed for emergent Hispanic readers and students learning Spanish in the United States. Simple stories and concepts are paired with photographs of real kids in real-life situations. Sentences are short and simple, employing a basic vocabulary of sight words, as well as new words that describe familiar things and places. With their engaging stories and vivid photo-illustrations, PowerKids *en español* gives children the opportunity to develop a love of reading and learning that they will carry with them throughout their lives.